Copeland's Daughter
Stephanie Conn

smith|doorstop

Published 2016 by
smith|doorstop books
The Poetry Business
Bank Street Arts
32–40 Bank Street
Sheffield S1 2DS

Copyright © Stephanie Conn 2016
All Rights Reserved

ISBN 978-1-910367-64-3
Typeset by Utter
Printed by People for Print, Sheffield

smith|doorstop books are a member of Inpress:
www.inpressbooks.co.uk. Distributed by Central Books
Ltd., 99 Wallis Road, London E9 5LN

The Poetry Business gratefully acknowledges the support of
Arts Council England.

Contents

3	The First Lighthouse
4	Walled Garden
5	Carved in Stone
6	Copeland's Daughter
8	Wedding Night
9	Have You Ever Heard the Like
10	Winter
12	Making Butter
13	Fish Trap
14	Molly and the Islanders
16	Her Precious Cargo
17	The Islanders' New Clothes
18	Esther
19	The Last to Leave
22	St. Brendan's Floating Isle
24	Testing the Theory
26	Uprooted
27	On Visiting the Island of my Ancestors
28	Gull Egg Season
29	Hidden Trails
30	Family Line
32	On your birthday
33	August 25th

for my father

The First Lighthouse
Cross Island, 1714

Even then, the flaming beacon was old-fashioned;
lensed lamps had been available for years, yet
an open-fire blazed on top of the white-washed tower;

three storeys of island-quarried stone, picked
and carried on the convicts' backs.
They built the walls two metres thick.

These twenty acres never did attract the sun;
there was no call for a mirror to catch the light:
Alexandria's blue skies were little more than fables.

The people here had no time for sea-gods
who shepherd seals or speak of the past or future;
in these parts, that is better left unsaid.

This land lies three miles from the Lough's mouth,
knows nothing of the Nile's flat plains or
the limestone pharos, reinforced with molten lead.

But yes, the fires burned alike. An iron spindle,
twenty metres up, revolved beneath the brazier;
the hot coals kept burning by the keeper –

a ton and a half on a windy night;
the old donkey lugging the black stuff
up the hill from the moonlit beach.

Walled Garden

To live on a small patch of flat land,
in the middle of the sea, you need defences.
If herbs and fruit trees are to grow,
if you want chicken flavoured with rosemary
or poached pears and blackberries,
you must build four walls, raise the temperature
by degrees, to coax saplings to the sky.
The stone absorbs what little heat the sun gives,
prevents frost forming on fuchsia
flowered currants and salt-laden iced winds
from battering the swelling fruit.
There is nothing ornamental about this square
of stone built so close to waves
churning up porcelain and flakes of skin.

Carved in Stone

Having built four sturdy walls, block
by chiselled block, in the August heat,
the stone masons left the space inside,
paced, instead, the acres of rank grass
and bracken towards the east cliff.

Leaving the birds to the air they kneeled,
as if in prayer, to inspect the layered rock –
white veins of calcite and quartz, fine-grained
sandstone, grey with fragments and feldspar –
rubbed with one thumb and then another.

They traced a single glinting line to the cave,
pressed weathered hands against the inner wall's
rough edges, its indentations damp as November
and just as dull. In that hollow chamber, stooped
to carve two names in the sea's abandoned rock.

Copeland's Daughter

> *Queen ants unhook their wings, post-flight, to find a permanent nest.*

Lifting her tightly-stitched skirts,
she stepped on board her father's boat,
glancing back at a pair of arctic tern.

As kids they knew the call of every Copeland bird.
In the schoolroom they'd longed to be knee-deep
in some rock-pool or skimming stones on the shore.

They learned each inch of land by heart
and from his house on the hill they'd watched
the others leave, rolling their eyes in secret.

She crossed the Sound in silence, listening
to the waves, until the noise of feet and voice
announced dry land. Strangers congregated

on the streets of Donaghadee to see them pass.
She looked to the hills. On the road to Ards
the wheels caught, spluttering dirt and dust,

and she glimpsed the path her brothers took.
Green fields stretched in every direction;
here, blue was reserved for sky.

In the windowless room forget-me-nots
drooped in the August heat. A puddle sat
in the pit of a small well, black and thick.

She took his hand, for this was what she knew;
before speech or sense of home, she knew this face,
this look. They signed their names in ink.

Wedding Night

Under thatch they
searched for new land.
He skimmed surface –
touched hair, face, lips.

Discovered place
in curve of breast
and thigh, felt the
rise and fall of breath.

Entered sea and
sky and stars, found
her in August
moonlight, shining.

He held her gaze –
you are my island.

Have You Ever Heard the Like

She has called on a dowser;
brought him to the island
to find water on our Jim's land,
so they can sink a well.
The young pups not fit to walk
a half-mile to fill their buckets
and us doing it our whole lives.

Him with his forked stick,
walking slowly around the field,
it bending for every hidden stream;
the oul boy knowing from the tilt
how deep the water ran, how close
to the surface, and every place he stood
provided, till the eejits feared a flood.

Winter

We are cut off from the mainland again;
a pile of unopened letters sits in Donaghadee;
there is flour and salt and treacle in the grocer's,
bags of coal and paraffin to fill the empty tins,
but the boat keeps close to the harbour wall.

Tide in, tide out and the beam of light,
and a distant moon – waxing and waning.

Still, the bread is baked and the butter churned,
the blocken cured and the rabbits trapped,
mussels are plucked from the island pools
and pickled in jars on larder shelves.
The firewood and driftwood is stacked.

Tide in, tide out and the beam of light,
and a distant moon – waxing and waning.

Inside the lamps are lit and curtains pulled,
while out at sea, the wind and waves confront
each other in torrents of eddies and pools
and the gulls circling above the spume
could be vultures in the thick sea-mist.

Tide in, tide out and the beam of light,
and a distant moon – waxing and waning.

But we know what the darkness brings;
it drags us from sleep into nightmare, lost in fog
we'll be struck by ship after floundering ship;
forced into the driving rain, where muffled voices call
from their wreck. We'll run to the shore to save all we can.

Tide in, tide out and the beam of light,
and a distant moon – waxing and waning.

In a place such as this, we are used to the ghosts,
but not to their dying; never to the bodies of young men
washed up on the shore, with their puffed up faces
and gaping sockets where the eyes should be; or the tiny crab
emerging from a silenced mouth to scurry, ever sideways.

Making Butter

At 5am the four-foot churn is pulled from the garden,
where sun and wind have kept the milk sweet;
the hour will keep it cool. Her utensils are gleaming,
salt-scrubbed and scalded, resting in cold water
carried up from the well in the lower field.

I ask to drop the skimmed cream into the churn.
She lets me watch. The heavy dash starts to rise
and fall – slowly at first, slow-ly, slow-ly, then faster.
I count fifty lifts a minute, then fifty more, and more
until my head is dizzy with it, and I fear I will faint,

knowing I will lie here on the cement floor till
the butter's come. I wish she'd sing a churning song
to pass the time until the mixture breaks. She works it silently.
At last she stops to wash her hands as a surgeon would,
lowers them into steaming water that should scald her skin.

She doesn't flinch but scoops up the creamy sunshine
in her glowing hands, cleans it four times, salts it, shapes it
into half pound pats. When she turns her back I press in the print
of a thistle, feel my fingers sink just as easily as a blade might
and when she turns around I am shoving them into my mouth.

Fish Trap

It is not my job to mind this lower land.
I should be on the southern shore
collecting sea-wrack for the upper fields,
not crouching out of sight, watching men
bent double at Port Ramon, constructing
their stone trap in the shallow inlet –
a long linear strip of stacked rock, to meet,
at an oblique angle, this shorter arm,
perfectly set to catch fish on the falling tide.

I learned that Pollock feed over wrecks,
have a preference for ragged sea-beds,
feed on sprat, small mackerel, sand-eels,
dive to avoid our nets and rods, outsmart
us in the tangled kelp. My father calls
them fighting fish. I nod in time with him.

At night, after the candles are blown out,
I see their massive mouths, protruding jaws,
the staring eyes. With mine pressed shut
it's easier to pick out the lateral line, silver
and curving upwards, the three dorsal fins.
In the sea their flanks are brown or greenish-grey
but in my hands their backs are shining copper,
their bellies white, and sliced and oozing
iridescent flesh and fine bones that pierce my feet.

Molly and the Islanders

True, I had no claim to the land
and a rough sea made me nervous.
Still, I thought I could live like them.

I did not know each plaidy or rock-bush
up and down the Sound, but learned
to grease and roll the timbers so the keel
could glide over them, knew to stack
the precious loans well above high water.

When rain poured through the roof's crack,
soaking the hay-filled mattress, we slept
upside-down, feet covered in an oil cloth coat.
When the draughts blew through the open
chimney we sat by the fire wrapped in blankets.
We learned to live in a house made up of narrow
spaces: took care of elbows, hot coals on the range,
ducked under ceilings, grew accustomed to ourselves.

I knew it wasn't all willows and blackberry bushes,
golden whin and wild narcissi; the coo-loo of curlews
circling over the walnut tree. There were dykes to re-build,
twenty acres of brambles to clear, a small walled garden
to bring back to cultivation; work that required more
than bread and tea.When I wasn't clipping or dipping,
I carried buckets across the wind-battered fields, hearing
only the cries of bereaved ewes as their lambs took to the sea.

I spoke too much, got to the point too soon, came down with fevers,
believed the post-box plaque, pressed into the rock, when it announced
'next collection Monday', and on the day the bullock got itself stuck
fast in the sheugh, I watched them fetch the rope, helped them pass
it between his twitching shoulders and the soft earth, felt the pull
and haul, the twisting weight of it, in my blistered hands. I knew then
that the poor beast had wandered off course, was never meant
to find itself stranded in a narrow gully on such steep sloping land.

Her Precious Cargo

The wind was up and making a mockery
of our makeshift defences, when the boys came running,
arms flailing and bodies tilted towards the ground,
as they rushed head-first at the wind. The wind
that swallowed the words from their open mouths,
whipped their cheeks, snatched at their coats,
splattered hair to their faces in the lashing rain.

And I, so full of the next one I could barely move,
forcing myself from the kitchen sink to undo the latch.
The door caught fast and slammed against brick
while above the thatch was in full rebellion.
I saw it before the boys reached the house –
cloud upon billowing white cloud, amidst the storm's
black sky, and then the almighty crack as she struck the rock.

Faces at the cottage doors and the men running through fields
towards the cobbled shore, to the crash of masts,
the creak and snap of shrouds and stays,
and the flap of sails thundering over wind.
And inside me the swell and thud of a twisting child,
as an elbow, foot or shoulder, nudges at my ribs –
they pass me by as I rest between shallow breaths.

Our men take in the sight of the sheer and sweeping lines;
her high arched stern and lofty spars, broken
and drooping before their eyes. They launch the yawl
and labour to reach these drowning men, who rate ship
over sea, wit against wind, vanity over cold hard rock.
And now she's split, she's torn in two –
spilling her cargo into the sea and turning the tide red.

The Islanders' New Clothes

Wild with rage and waving a loaded gun
the Captain spun from left to right, despite
the water rushing in to soak his feet,
heat rising from his damp brow and flushed cheeks.
On the tee-side three passengers jumped ship,
less concerned with cloth and silk than their own
necks. Each coaxed from the yawl as the Clipper
slipped lower in the swelling, northern tide.
In the end he leapt from the shaking deck.
The fearless sea crashed, ripped her to ruin
leaving only bow by lamp-lighting time.
Armed guards could barely gather the littered
bales stacked on the rocks and the satin sand,
left bright sleeves rustling above weathered hands.

Esther

For years my body grew taut, then slack,
as each child filled me to the point of breathlessness;
jabbing my middle, pressing out the skin
in tiny hand or foot shaped pouches.

When they sucked at the breast, my belly
dragged itself back in, to a strange new shape;
their pursed lips surrounded by a dark sun
grown twice its normal size –

and each time a new baby latched on,
I caught my breath; the slitting pain of that first
suck, searing to my stomach's pit,
following the fine line of black hair

that doesn't have time to fade between births.
As though my smooth centre belonged only
to childhood, and becoming a woman
brings downy hairs to the face.

I barely had time to bleed, would happily
have washed the stained sheets he liked to keep
white, and pegged them to dry above the freesia
looking out to see which field he had left fallow.

The Last to Leave

Out in the yard
they are selling our lives,
and the gavel drops –
while he sits inside
stoking the fire,
fixated on the flame.

When the time comes,
he steps into the boat
without looking back –
and sits by my side,
not saying a word.
He can't meet my eyes.

My own eyes fall
to the thick wooden slats
and the iron bolts
that keep me afloat,
above the currents
swirling on the Sound.

If only it were night,
I would look up at the stars
my father named for me
sixty years ago or more,
lifting me onto his shoulders
so I could touch the sky.

I would throw up my hands
and release them all;
clutter the sky
with island parts
and name them
one by one.

Not just the Plough
but the sickle and scythe,
the pitchfork and hoe,
the threshing mill.
Yellow iris, saltmarsh, turf,
stonecrop, bracken, inland cliff.

My manx shearwater,
black headed gull,
arctic tern and eider duck,
stock dove, gannet, lapwing, nest.
Schoolhouse, cottage, garden gate,
boatman, teacher, daughter, son –

the children,
all of our children.
Cassiopeia,
what have you lost?
Oh Cephes, who ties
their daughter to a rock?

But the sun is high,
the stars have gone out
and the boat is set to tip,
so I drop the Copeland
pebbles, one by one,
and watch them sink.

St. Brendan's Floating Isle

Fed up to the back teeth
trying to swallow my tail,
I took to watching islands;

small figures on the beach
hauling nets, eating together
on the sand; telling stories.

It is not easy being at sea.
Some days the sun makes
my scales shine and quiver

but in truth they are grey,
and there is nothing to do
but dive into the ink swell

feeling the currents' tug;
so when I saw them coming
I paid attention –

skin stretched over wooden ribs,
tar smeared where the hides met
and the strange scent of oak bark;

voices carried like salt in the wind,
making my eyes sting, the lilting
sound was an unknown symphony

and the sight of those men side
by side, oars in their skelfed hands,
was all it took to draw me in.

I kept myself still, as though
twisted roots held me to the sea bed,
and lowered my head as if in prayer,

longing to feel their feet on my bare
back, exploring my shoreless edges
to translate their talk into glorious kinship.

I did not know it would burn;
the warmth of their heavy limbs
turned to fire and I cast them off.

Testing the Theory

The year I was born you sailed the Atlantic,
in a hand-crafted boat, to see if it was possible;

a replica of Brendan's sixth century curragh,
accurately reconstructed with traditional tools,

built of Irish oak and ash; curved frame
of bone-white wood, hand-lashed together

in two miles of leather thong; this relic
of the Stone Age wrapped tightly in forty-nine

tanned ox hides and sealed with sheep wool
grease. You went to sea in search of the truth.

~

The slim shadow of an improbable vessel,
her tapering bow, her stern rising gently;

the thin skin, a quarter of an inch thick,
flexing and shifting in a most peculiar motion

– heave, sway, bob, sway, heave – her sides
pumping softly, in and out, as if breathing.

As you approached each mapped island cluster,
square sails tied taut, the celtic crosses shining

crimson, did the island folk see you coming?
Note the collapse of flax beyond the harbour?

~

In the turmoil of an ocean gale
did you count the waves, fearing

the seventh, knowing the oceanographers
called it superstition, having their laws

of wave mechanics, the sea's surface
receptive only to chaotic wind drag?

But what of huge pillars of floating crystal,
fire breathing monsters or flaming rocks?

Nothing at all to report but active volcanoes and ice,
and a phial of holy water stowed inside the gunwale.

Uprooted

This huge tree, done with tolerating gales
on open land, has tilted towards the ground –
three-quarters of her ancient roots exposed
like the coloured frills of a can-can skirt.

The sycamore withstands sea-spray,
produces winged seeds, wood for sailors'
love-spoons, but little in the way of folklore;
it bends above grass at a thirty degree angle.

The rhizome mass of roots is meant
for underground; subterranean stems
best kept out of sight in the dark soil,
not for air that turns the twisting grey.

The witch's bone-dry fingers grip
lumps of rock and glass, chunks
of metal, forgotten trinkets. A thin
fraction of the tree clings on, ignores

the crumbling bark, the strange incline –
draws water from a narrow stream, sends
it to the upper leaves, along the radiating
veins to the ragged edge; keeps them green.

On Visiting the Island of my Ancestors

A hand gripped, then pulled, to lift my body
from the boat. My foot finds the moving metal
grille, slips on sea-green fibres. I watch my step.

The land is cushion-soft and punctured by rabbit holes.
The field by the shore sprouts patches of rigid grass
and bluebells. On the hill there is a scattering

of broken shell and bone. The skull of a small bird,
stripped bare, reveals teeth at the end of the beak,
eye-socket shaped spaces. The brain's imprint remains.

A single step is enough to send a flock of black-
capped Eider duck to the sky, their green napes
flashing. Their cries are long and hoarse.

I taste salt at the back of my throat, raise cold hands
to my ears to drown out the screech the gulls
are making, keep clear of the south-facing cliffs;

the dive and swoop and squawk of them draws me in.
Exposed nests litter the rocks, soften the lichen-covered
ridges, hold blue-grey speckled eggs, in threes.

Five steps back, and silent, I watch one crack –
see shadows shift behind the splitting case, before
a tiny beak emerges – opens and closes, opens again.

Gull Egg Season

The eggs of a black-headed gull are difficult to see in daylight:
speckled pale-blue shell and just a hint of green on the smooth
ovoid; high glossed, and fragile as a new-born's fontanelle.

Herbaceous mats rest in the scraped ground. Above the nest
cup, the male takes the night-shift, incubates the clutch,
lulled by the glow of artificial light rising from the mainland.

This island's rocks are treacherous, the sea-mists distort distance
and the tide's currents churn to their own erratic rhythm, forcing
local boats along specific paths, sails pulled at just the right point.

Hessian rustles against thick-set thighs. Twine unravels in a pocket,
discarding fibre. A sudden thud, the rush and flap of wings colliding;
a callous call, crying out from unhinged jaws as the colony empties.

At Treasure Cove, by candlelight, gull eggs fetch ten pounds each.
Served up on a terracotta plate, seasoned with a sprinkling of celery salt,
they are split in two and sliced to reveal the still moist, orange-red yolk.

Hidden Trails

Navigating these underground tunnels
isn't easy now they've fallen in,
but if by chance, in a dream, you pass
through the toppled stone and find yourself
inside a chamber built of brick, slip down
the subterranean corridor and wait,
wait for the whisperers to return,
suddenly glad of prying ears and thudding hearts,
albeit slowed by sleep, and smell the air
turn acrid with tobacco and gin.
Breathe, take it all in before you wake.
Perhaps these forgotten paths that lead to the sea
are nothing but drains, and the footsteps
you heard were just an echo of your own.

Family Line

When we meet at the harbour wall
neither of us mention the date
though you hug me tightly.

Nineteen years and not counting.
We climb down uneven steps
and clamber onto the boat.

At this speed we will be there
in ten minutes or less; six hundred
seconds until we disembark.

The wind presses our faces into strange
shapes, snatches the questions
from my salt-laced mouth.

You taught me to skim stones;
now you reach out your hand
to steady me on the jagged rocks.

We follow the island rules; keep to the edges.
You estimate the distance to the mainland;
the stretch your brother never swam.

You prefer cold facts to stories; like to list
the names of flowers and birds, can easily
distinguish male from female,

delight at the sight of wobbling chicks,
ill-disguised to your well trained eye.
The parents shriek. You drew me ducks

on notepads and napkins, taught me to dive.
I explain who is who in the crowded graveyard –
how exactly you descend from those laid here.

I lead you inland, point out the smaller islands.
One turn and all is overgrown. You beat a path
through sharp grass, keep clear of the thistles

and yellow wild flowers. You watch seal heads
emerge beyond the headland; something glints
on the brink - three white deck chairs in a row.

On your birthday

The boatman will return at two. For now,
I am alone on this sponge-sprung island,
finding my way over slate and shingle,
following the sand track to the graveyard.
There is a small gap in the low stone wall –
did a gate once fill the space I pass through?
This soft land is falling in on itself.
Beside stone markers, headstones tilt into
each other, making it difficult to read
the chiselled details of my ancestors.
Above a labyrinth of rabbit holes,
I wonder where the fur-lined tunnels lead,
trace names and dates with shaking fingers,
snag skin – you did not get to be this old.

August 25th

A good day for starting out, or so it seemed
to the Royal Society who sent Cook sailing

off into the Atlantic, round Cape Horn, journeying
westwards to Tahiti to record the Transit of Venus.

And Webb agreed; diving off Admiralty Pier,
smeared in porpoise oil, to swim the Channel;

keeping his stroke steady, despite the jellyfish stings,
the churning currents off Cap Gris Nez, to Calais.

A bride's dress rests below the collar bone,
covers pale skin, tightens at the waist.

The gladioli stems are wrapped in green satin
to draw out the glint of peridot at her neck.

A gold band placed on her steady finger
is loose enough to pass over the knuckle.

She will search out the star-maiden in the sky,
follow a small black disc across the moon's face.

Gallileo offers up his newly ground lenses.
The lawmakers ascend the city belltowers,

lift the telescope to their eyes to see the sails
of distant ships, distinct and impossibly close.

Voyager 2 draws as close as it has ever been
to Saturn's rings of ice-particles and dust,

ammonia crystals create a pale yellow glow
in the dark space where sixty-two moons orbit.

Her great-grandchild wears crushed silk,
exposing sun-blushed skin, thin wrists.

The gaping heads of lilac poppies
lie against her trussed up breasts.

There is an exchange of white-gold rings.
Her body is cloaked in sweat and trembling.

The black sky shines with a thousand
stars that burned out years ago.

Acknowledgements

Acknowledgements are due to the editors of the following publications in which some of these poems first appeared: *Abridged*, *Banshee*, *Burning Bush 2*, *Connections* (Community Arts Partnership Anthology), *Elbow Room*, *Honest Ulsterman*, *Irish Examiner*, *North West Words*, *On the Grass When I Arrive* (Guildhall Anthology) *Shift*, *Southword* and *The Sea* (RNLI Anthology)

An earlier version of 'Making Butter' won the Yeovil Poetry Prize in 2015.

'Gull Egg Season' was highly commended in the Gregory O'Donoghue Competition, 2015.

I am grateful to the Arts Council of Northern Ireland for a Career Enhancement Award in 2014. Thanks are due to Damian Smyth and Moyra Donaldson for their support and encouragement; to Emma Must for her invaluable feedback and believing in the poems; to Johnny Conn for proofreading with such care, and to all those with connections to the Copeland Islands and Donaghadee who helped me reveal the story of my ancestors.

LOTTERY FUNDED